A LOVE LIKE NO OTHER

Joyful Reflections from the Hearts of Mothers

COMPILED BY
ELISA MORGAN
PRESIDENT, MOPS INTERNATIONAL

PAINTINGS BY
LAURIE SNOW HEIN

A LOVE LIKE NO OTHER: JOYFUL REFLECTIONS FROM THE HEARTS OF MOTHERS
©2002 by MOPS International, Inc.
published by Multnomah Publishers, Inc.
P.O. Box 1720, Sisters, OR 97759

ISBN 1-57673-913-9

MOPS International

MOPS (Mothers of Preschoolers) is a program designed to encourage mothers with children under school age through relationships and resources. Approximately 2,700 MOPS groups gather in churches throughout the United States, Canada, and thirteen other countries to meet the needs of more than 100,000 women each year. The women are of many ages and backgrounds but share the same desire—to be the best mothers they can be.

Find out how MOPS International can help you become part of the
MOPS ❤ to ❤ Mom Connection.

MOPS International
P.O. Box 102200
Denver, CO 80250-2200
Phone 1-800-929-1287 or 303-733-5353
E-mail: Info@MOPS.org
Web site: http://www.MOPS.org

Artwork©Arts Uniq®, Inc.
Artwork designs by Laurie Snow Hein are reproduced under license from Arts Uniq®, Inc., Cookeville, Tennessee, and may not be reproduced without permission. For information regarding art prints featured in this book, please contact:

Arts Uniq®, Inc.
P.O. Box 3085
Cookeville, TN 38502
1-800-223-5020

Published in association with the literary agency of:
Alive Communications, Inc.
7680 Goddard Street, Suite 200
Colorado Springs, CO 80920

Design by Koechel Peterson & Associates, Minneapolis, Minnesota

Multnomah Publishers, Inc., has made every effort to trace the ownership of all poems and quotes. In the event of a question arising from the use of a poem or quote, we regret any error made and will be pleased to make the necessary correction in future editions of this book.

Please see the acknowledgments at the back of the book for complete attributions for this material.

Scripture quotations are taken from *The Holy Bible*, New International Version © 1973, 1984 by International Bible Society, used by permission of Zondervan Publishing House; *The Living Bible* (TLB) © 1971, used by permission of Tyndale House Publishers. All rights reserved.

CONTENTS

INTRODUCTION

When a child is born, a mother is born. And when a mother is born, a unique and powerful love grows from the center of her heart and reaches out, across years and through all obstacles, to shape the life of her child. It's a love that is inspiring, incredible, and invincible. It's a love like no other.

The seeds of this love are planted long before birth—perhaps that first moment when a little girl notices a mother caressing her baby, or when that little girl tucks her favorite baby doll into a toy crib for the first time. The seeds grow as the little girl grows, as she dreams of being a mother with babies of her own.

A mother recognizes this amazing, enduring love for her baby in their first gentle embrace and is astonished to feel it expand during all the moments that follow: when she softly sings a lullaby while cradling her baby in her arms…when she carefully tugs tiny arms and legs into cozy pajamas…as she watches a sleepy yawn interrupt a late-night feeding.

And then this wondrous love blossoms even more as the child grows up. The mother gives hugs of healing after a scraped knee…cries when a dandelion is taped to a rock and presented to her on Mother's Day…marches her six-year-old up to a neighbor's door so that he might apologize for scalping every single spring tulip from that neighbor's flower bed…prays for safety on the night of her "baby's" first solo drive, and beams with pride at each of her child's achievements, both large and small.

Come! Celebrate with me in this love like no other, and treasure these joyful reflections of every mother's heart. In them, I hope you'll find delight in your own remembrances from your journey of motherhood.

Elisa Morgan

Elisa Morgan
President, MOPS International

I'll Love You Forever

Every mother's story is unique, and every mother's love for her child incomparable. Yet this incredible, invincible love also binds mothers together. We share a devotion that "always protects, always trusts, always hopes, always perseveres." As you savor each tender word in the pages ahead, consider the enduring strength of a mother's love. Like eternity, it's a love that lasts forever.

❋ ❋ ❋

You're not sure about this little being inside of you who's draining your energy and kicking your ribs. The months pass quickly with baby showers, friendly pats on your belly, and questions about whether it's a boy or a girl. Your mother wants to know: Will you breastfeed or bottle-feed? How about Thea for a name? Then, one day, the contractions hit. Your water breaks. You check your bags one more time, grab the birthing book, and waddle to the car while your husband asks for the hundredth time, "Are you okay?"

A mother is the only person on earth who can divide her love among all her children and each child still have all her love.

—Author unknown

❄ ❄ ❄

Later—was it twenty minutes or twenty hours? you hear the cry and the doctor announces, "It's a boy." This is the moment your heart expands to a size you never thought possible. He's placed in your arms, this small and innocent child, a gift from God. You feel his soft cheek against your skin. You gently pull him closer. And you whisper: "I'll love you forever."

—**Angela Dean Lund**, Sisters, Oregon

WHEN IS A MOTHER BORN? I WAS BORN A mother with the first echoes of my baby's heartbeat. Though not yet in my arms, my infant's heart called to me, bringing out in me the need to love and protect, to cherish and encourage. With each kick and roll, tuck and twirl, the life dancing inside me confirmed what I had just discovered— a mother is born the moment she feels the love in her heart for a child she has never seen.

—**Theresa Meyers**, Port Orchard, Washington

NOT TOO LONG AGO, MY DAUGHTER, THEN four years old, ran up to me and said, "Mommy, I love you more than I can." It brought tears to my eyes because that's exactly how I feel about her.

—**Pam Svoboda**, McCook, Nebraska

"Mother" means selfless devotion, limitless sacrifices,

and love that passes understanding.

—Author unknown

❊   ❊   ❊

WHEN I WAS A CHILD, MY MOTHER'S LAP WAS the warmest and safest place in the world. On my mother's lap, all the troubles of childhood would fade away, and I would be perfectly secure and content. I remember simply sitting on her lap for long periods of time. I suspect she had dishes to do, clothes to wash, errands to run, and yet, I sat. But I do not recall her ever telling me she had something to tend to. In fact, it was always I who ventured off first. Perhaps I had finally awakened from sleep, or my childhood hurts had been comforted away, but when I was emotionally full, I got up.

A mother's lap is a child's sanctuary.

—Carla Risener Bresnahan
Orlando, Florida

"I'M GOING HOME!"

The announcement came from two houses down, where four-year-old Madeline was playing on the sidewalk with her neighborhood buddies. Sharon, sitting on the front steps, looked up from her magazine and watched as her daughter stomped up the street toward her. She soon plopped down on the step next to her, folded her chubby little arms across her chest, and stuck out her bottom lip, the way she did when she was determined not to cry.

"They don't like me," she told her mother. "They won't let me play with them." With those words, her tears came, streaking dirt down her cherub cheeks.

"Tell me what happened, pumpkin," Sharon prompted as she wrapped her arm around the child.

Madeline gulp-sobbed her way through an explanation. "Jacob wouldn't let me carry his flashlight! He said I was too little and I might break it! He's so mean, Mommy! I'm not too little!" Exhausted from this outburst, she collapsed into the hollow of her mother's arm.

Sharon stroked her child's hair. It was so painful to see her daughter rejected and misunderstood like this. Another reminder that, as a mom, she couldn't prevent the wounds her child would experience in the world. But maybe she could soften their impact with love and encouragement.

Scooping Madeline up into her lap, Sharon gently brushed her daughter's hair away from her sticky cheeks and kissed her forehead. Then she perched her daughter on her knees, held her hands, and looked straight into her wide, sad eyes, eyeball to eyeball.

"Madeline, do you know how wonderful you are?" she asked.

Madeline shook her head and pulled a hand free to wipe her eyes.

"Madeline, you are the most wonderfulest

girl in the whole wide world! I love your button nose." Sharon smooched it quickly. "I love your cherry red cheeks." She pecked them and continued. "I love your eyelashes and your adorable little eary ears." She bestowed kisses on her daughter's eyes and ears. "I love you from the top of your head all the way down to your twinkly little toes." She bent Madeline's head forward for a kiss and then picked up sandaled feet and smooched her dimpled toes. "I love your heart," pointing at her chest, "your kindness, your fun ideas, your sweet little sharing spirit."

Madeline stopped crying and watched her mother, wide-eyed. She hung on to every word, giggled through the kisses, and eagerly followed from one affirmation to the next. Hungry from her very soul for these endearments, she opened, like a baby bird, to receive her mother's nurture.

Finally Sharon hugged her daughter close to her chest. "Oh, Madeline," she exclaimed, "I'm absolutely crazy about you!"

—Elisa Morgan, Denver, Colorado,

and Carol Kuykendall, Boulder, Colorado

The loveliest masterpiece of the heart of God is the heart of a mother.

—Thérèse of Lisieux

A mother is a person who sees that there are only four pieces of pie for five persons and promptly remarks that she's never cared for pie.

—Author unknown

I REALIZED AFTER THE FIRST FEW DAYS that this was what I had been waiting for and working toward all of my life. Nothing else I had done, or would ever do, would be as important or perfect as having this child and being this child's mother forever.

—Janet Chambers, Davis, California

"BYE, I LOVE YOU!" MY CHILDREN SHOUT TO me as they leave for school in the mornings. It warms my heart to know that my kids are not ashamed to tell the world that they love me. May it always be so.

—Linda Crawford, San Diego, California

14

Beat upon mine, little heart! Beat! Beat!

Beat upon mine! You are mine, my sweet!

All mine from your pretty blue eyes to your feet, my sweet!

—Alfred Tennyson

❋ ❋ ❋

WHEN I WAS PREGNANT WITH YOU, MY second child, I was a bit worried that there was not enough of my heart left for you. I was totally and completely in love with your brother, my first child. Then you were born and I soon learned that a mother's heart grows with each new child. I love you both in individual ways because you are unique, yet the love I feel for you both is intensely the same.

—Sarah Keeton, Sisters, Oregon

BEFORE YOU CAME, I KNEW THAT I WOULD love you. I knew that there was room in my heart for you. But I thought that it would take time for us to bond, that my love for you would grow a little each day. After all, that's how love is supposed to happen.

What a surprise! They brought you to me for the very first time. As I held you and looked into the gaze of your newborn eyes, I knew that I had been wrong. My love for you is complete.

—Patricia Sprinkle, Miami, Florida

ARRIVING HOME FROM THE HOSPITAL WITH our newborn baby, I looked into the backseat at him strapped into his car seat and thought, I hardly know you, but I would die for you right now if I had to. It was precisely at that moment that I understood the true meaning of unconditional love. It was then that I understood how much God loves me.

—Carla Schneider, Sisters, Oregon

A mother's love! What can compare with it!

Of all things on earth, it comes nearest to divine love in heaven.

A mother's love means a life's devotion—

And sometimes a life's sacrifice—

With but one thought, one hope, and one feeling,

That her children will grow up healthy and strong,

Free from evil habits and able to provide for themselves.

—Author unknown

HUSH MY PRECIOUS LITTLE ONE,
And give to me a smile.
I've heard your cry. I know your need.
Let's sit and rock awhile.
I'll hold you in my arms so tight
    and sing a lullaby.
You need not fear, I'm always near
    the apple of my eye.

—Rebecca Stephens, Conifer, Colorado

NO ONE COULD HAVE PREPARED ME FOR
this. Nothing I had read or seen could describe the
exquisite joy of my soul. I'm a mother! Me! Oh
heart, be still. Who is this sweet, pink face—so fresh
from heaven—peeking out from beneath her
blanket cocoon? Oh, God, you have such faith and
trust in me. Please stay close and whisper in my ear
the things I need to know. I want to do my best.

—Kathy Erickson, Freedom, Wyoming

* * *

A wonderful being is a mother. Other folks may love you,

but only your mother understands. Mothers work for you,

care for you, love, and forgive you. And when you leave her,

like a guardian angel, her memory is always with you.

—Author unknown

YOU BRING ME SUCH JOY

Can anything compare to the simple delight of a tiny hand wrapped around your finger, or a morning's first smile that reaches into your soul? Our children have a special gift for giving wings to our spirits. Read on and let each expression of a mother's joy warm your heart as you reflect on the soaring moments in your life.

I came rushing through our dining room in my best suit, focused on getting ready for an evening meeting. Gillian, my four-year-old, was dancing about to one of her favorite oldies.

I was in a hurry, on the verge of being late. Yet a small voice inside of me said, *Stop.*

So I stopped. I looked at her. I reached out, grabbed her hand, and spun her around. My seven-year-old came into our orbit, and I grabbed her, too. The three of us did a wild jitterbug around the dining room and into the living room. We were laughing. We were spinning.

The song ended with a dramatic flourish and our dance finished with it. I patted them on their bottoms and sent them to take their baths.

They went up the stairs, gasping for breath,

their giggles bouncing off the walls. I was bent over, shoving papers into my briefcase, when I overheard my youngest say to her sister, "Caitlin, isn't Mommy the bestest one?"

I froze. How close I had come to hurrying through life, missing that moment. My mind went to the awards and diplomas that covered the walls of my office. No award, no achievement can ever match these words: *Isn't Mommy the bestest one?*

It doesn't fit on my résumé. But I want it on my tombstone.

—Gina Barrett Schlesinger
Philadelphia, Pennsylvania

SLIPPING HIS SMALL HAND INTO MY OPEN palm, he simultaneously fills my hand and heart.

— Barbi Townsend, Newport Beach, California

RAISING A CHILD—TEACHING, ENCOURAGING, disciplining—through all this, does he know I love him? This morning I received my answer. My rambunctious toddler crawled into my lap, and laying the sweetest of kisses on my cheek, said, "Momma, you're my best friend."

My heart is still singing.

— Dawn Lewis, Glendora, California

I WAS THERE WHEN THEY WOKE, PLAYED, ate, cried, laughed, needed clean diapers, and went to sleep. I kissed them just for pure joy.

—Juanita Tamayo Lott
Silver Spring, Maryland

The laugh of a child.

Love it, I love it, the laugh of a child.

Now rippling and gentle, now merry and wild;

Ringing out on the air with its innocent gush;

Like the trill of a bird at the twilight's soft hush;

Floating off on the breeze, like the tones of a bell,

Or the music that dwells on the heart of a shell;

Oh! The laugh of a child, so wild and so free

Is the merriest sound in the world for me.

—Author unknown

I used to wonder if I'd feel like a mother when I finally became one. Both of my children were adopted. For Eva, we waited four and a half long years. Then Ethan joined us two and a half years later.

During those early waiting days I wondered just where God had gone. I'd go into the nursery, thunk the mattress, and watch the dust fly. It had been months since I'd wallpapered, made the bumper pads, and set out the stuffed animals to greet my little one.

One of those years, before Christmas, I decided to set up what we later called a "hope for the baby" tree. I tied pink and blue ribbons on the branches and tucked in pieces of baby's breath. Each day I prayed, "A baby by Christmas, please, God." But Christmas came and went without a little one.

It was the following April—the day before Easter—that my husband, Evan, and I received the call at last. I could hear Eva crying even before we entered the adoption agency. After all these years I was bursting to know her, love her, and mother her. Inside, we saw three-week-old Eva on a table—just a hard, folding table like you'd find in any school cafeteria. She was lying on a thin pink blanket, arms out, feet kicking slightly, and crying while the caseworker and foster mom talked and ignored her.

My heart twisted within me. *Someone pick up that baby! Someone hold her!*

I looked from caseworker to foster mom to my husband but the response came from within. *Well, I'm the mother.* I marched over, picked up Eva, and bonded with her on the spot. When Ethan was placed in my arms twenty-eight months later, my heart somersaulted into a love relationship with him, too.

I wondered if I'd feel like a mother when I became one. Indeed, I did. In a miraculous moment, God handed me one of His precious children and I was born: mother.

—Elisa Morgan, Denver, Colorado

AS I APPROACH MY TWO-YEAR-OLD SON'S bedroom this morning, it occurs to me that I am living out the Paradox of Motherhood. In the seconds it takes me to push open the door, two seemingly incongruous thoughts run through my mind: "Wow, I am just really, really tired, and it's going to be yet another day of diapers, discipline, meals, and messiness," followed immediately by, "I cannot wait to get to his bed and kiss him good morning and see what kinds of things he does today!"

The Paradox of Motherhood or, perhaps, in the end, the Paradise of Motherhood.

— Debbie Ricker, Sisters, Oregon

WHILE EXPECTING, I WAS ALWAYS TOLD MY life would be so different, but no one ever said how much better it would be.

—Tonya Roberts, Bardstown, Kentucky

MY BABY, KEARA, PLAYED WITH HER SOCKS while I read. After a few minutes, she started gurgling and laughing. I looked up and saw that she held her little yellow sock in her hand. It was her first catch. A proud moment. She tilted her head a bit, looked straight at me with a "watch this" kind of expression, and placed the sock on her head. She sat there staring at me with the sock on her head and the goofiest expression on her face, waiting for me to respond. I laughed with more spontaneity and joy than I'd felt in months. She took the sock off her head. Then she gave me the look again and put it back on. I laughed so hard my ribs hurt. Tears cascaded down my face. Again and again, she took the sock off and then put it back on her little bald head. And every time, I laughed more than the time before. It was our first true moment of shared joy.

—Martha Manning

BOUNDING IN, BURSTING WITH EXCITEMENT, bubbling with laughter, recounting her time away—I love the first few moments when my child returns after being gone.

—Mary Byrne Santori
Northridge, California

Love always protects.

— I Corinthians 13:7

IT WAS AN EXTRAORDINARY MOMENT AT THE end of an otherwise ordinary day.

I was walking down the hallway of our home when I came upon the sweetest sight I had ever seen: my three-year-old son brushing his teeth. No, it wasn't the fact that Parker was brushing his teeth; it was what he looked like at that moment. With the aid of his well-used footstool, he still had to stand on his tippy toes to barely see into the mirror. Clad only in his white T-shirt and "big boy" underwear, the little muscles in his calves were clearly outlined. He looked so small, so innocent and pure.

I froze in place. Looking on, I realized that someday that same precious little boy would probably be bigger than I was. *He* would be able to pick *me* up! So, I willed time to stand still for a few marvelous moments while I soaked up the memory of what he looked like up on his tiptoes.

I thought of going to get my camera to capture the moment forever, but I couldn't bear to turn away. Instead, I did what mothers have been doing for centuries. I took a picture with my heart.

—Vickey L. Banks
Oklahoma City, Oklahoma

"WHO DO YOU LOVE MOST?"
"I love both of you most."
"You can't love both of us most.
You have to love one of us more than the other."
"Okay, I love one of you more than the other."
"Which one, then?"
"Both of you?"
"I think you love her more than you love me."
"My sweetie, isn't this rather silly?
Is what you want for me to say that I love you most?"
"No! I want you to say that you love both of us most!"
"That's what I say!"
"Okay!"

—Madeleine L'Engle, New York, New York

YOU LEAD ME TO WONDER

Marvel...miracle...mystery. These all describe the awesome nature of a newborn baby in a mother's arms. Perhaps, however, wonder is best of all. For every child is a wonder, and, as you'll see in the next few pages, every child leads us to an enchanting place that fills us with wonder at what is and what is yet to be.

Breeze so thick with dandelion stars, I stick out my tongue to catch one, like a snowflake. I watch the children run together on the grassy hill, a school of fish weaving in unison. Someday you will be one of them, but now I blink back my disbelief and cherish my secret. I am pregnant with you.

— Eva McGinnis, Federal Way, Washington

DURING THE FIRST WEEKS I USED TO LIE long hours with my baby in my arms, watching her sleep, sometimes catching a gaze from her eyes, feeling very near the edge, the mystery, perhaps the knowledge of life.

— Isadora Duncan

The most powerful combination of emotions in the world

is not called out by any cosmic event,

nor is it found in novels or history books;

merely, it is found by a parent gazing down upon a sleeping child.

—Author unknown

"CHASE HANSON BOURKE, YOU'RE IN TROUBLE!"
I said, drawing on the memory of the voice my
mother had once used on me.

As I grabbed the paper towels and stamped
toward him, he looked up at me, and in a quiet
voice said, "I sorry."

I don't know where he'd learned to say it; it
was certainly the first time I'd heard it. But by the
look of utter repentance on his face, I knew he
understood the words. And, perhaps for the first
time, I understood them, too.

—**Dale Hanson Bourke**
Chevy Chase, Maryland

HOW SHORT A TIME SINCE
I bore you in womb, in arms, in heart.
My labor pains return

Each time you plunge
Head first into the world, my child.
You've come to go
From my lap, my knee, my side
But never from my love.
Like Abraham with Isaac
I give you up—I receive you again.
Forever, my child.

—**Vicki Huffman**, Nashville, Tennessee

I AM CONTINUALLY AMAZED THAT MY
children will lick floors, eat sand and bugs, float
toys in the toilet, and share slobbered pacifiers,
but will not eat breaded chicken, mashed potatoes,
or those little friggly things in the soup.

—**Wendy Hyatt**
Salem, New Hampshire

RACHEL CAME HOME FROM SCHOOL TODAY with Kristin's phone number memorized! This is a first. I watch her march to the portable phone and say the number aloud as she dials.

"Hello. This is Rachel Gunn. May I please speak to Kristin?"

She balances the phone on her shoulder, just the way I do, and begins to walk around the house. I don't look like that, do I?

"Hi, Kristin. It's Rachel." She opens the cupboard and checks for snacks, still balancing the phone.

"Nothing. What are you doing?"

She heads for the front porch with a handful of pretzels. I call out after her, "Would you like something to drink?"

She half turns and, with a sweet facial expression and a finger touched to her lips, silently motions for me not to interrupt her. Is that what I do?

I casually follow her to the porch and nestle on the wicker love seat. I begin flipping through a magazine. Rachel's eyes meet mine, and she gives me a "Don't you have anything better to do than follow me around all day?" look.

She speaks. Not to me, but to that invisible person on the phone. "I remember your number."

She checks the hanging petunias with her free hand to see if they need water. There she is, balancing the phone on her shoulder, clutching pretzels with her right hand, and fingering the soil with her left. Just like her mother.

"Well, that's all. I guess I'll see you tomorrow at school."

She wipes her muddy finger on a leaf, still balancing the phone. Then clutching her wad of pretzels, she pulls a wicker chair toward her with her foot just like I do.

"Okay. Bye."

I watch as Rachel pulls the phone away from her ear with her free hand, then catches a pretzel between her teeth and presses the "off" button with her nose. Just like I do.

"Do you know what?" I tell her as she joins me on the love seat and tries to fit her preadolescent body onto my lap. "Do you know that I think you're absolutely amazing?"

She smiles, kisses me on the tip of my nose, and says, "I know. That's 'cause I'm just like you."

—Robin Jones Gunn, Vancouver, Washington

A mother understands what a child does not say.

—Jewish Proverb

HOW FRUSTRATING IT IS TO HAVE YOU CRY for me every time I leave the room, and yet it makes me see that I have accomplished my goal. You are bonded to *me*. I am your relief of hunger and discomfort, your security when you are unsure, and your warmth when you are cold. In your mind, I am everything. What an honor to have someone need me so.

—**Sarah Keeton**, Sisters, Oregon

I ONCE READ AN ARTICLE THAT SAID A mother lion roars only when her cubs are in danger. These days I think of that mother lion, of how I am like her. Most of the time I try to remain calm as I raise my four children, but every now and again a fierce roar rumbles from within me.

—**Ann Marie Drop**, Iowa City, Iowa

WHEN WAS THE MAGICAL DAY, THE ONE when I became a mother? I'm not sure if it was the day my son was born, or the first time he said that enchanted word: Mommy. I think the reason I can't remember the specific moment I became a mother is because it's impossible to imagine not being one.

—**Diana Cash**, Yorktown, Virginia

AS MY DAUGHTER STIRS IN HER CRIB NEARBY, I find myself planning. On a midsummer evening before bedtime, that hour when it's still light but the world has turned a dreamy blue and no child wants to go to bed, I will carry her out to the pond behind her grandmother's house so she can listen to the peep-peep of tree frogs and smell the pine breeze and watch the fireflies glint under a thumbnail moon. Just before it's time to go back inside, I'll lean down and say something sensible,

I hope. And then it will happen, the enchantment, that strange alchemy that fixes a flash of life into memory, and suddenly the whole scene will be etched, complete, hers forever, and mine, too.

—Suzanne Berne, Boston, Massachusetts

ALL MOTHERS ARE LISTENERS. THERE IS A part of me that is always at attention. I listen for the tiny baby's sound rising out of his muffled bassinet in the darkened and closed bedroom upstairs. I listen even when I'm blocks away, laughing in a room full of hilarious guests, even though my child is in his own bed, his own room, protected by a baby sitter.

While listening to my husband recount his daily activities, I strain to hear (over the sound of the mixing bowl) the children running, the slamming of the refrigerator door, the water streaming from a faucet. And I often find myself saying, "I can't hear you, my darling. Speak a little louder."

I listen to the quiet breath of a sleeping household. Even in my own slumber, I listen for a cough. A cry propels me to a bedside after the interrupting dream has passed, making me wonder, a little bewildered, why I am standing alone in the dark, barefoot and cold.

I am always sorting out the sounds—sorting the crashes on the overhead floor from the squeaking of toys, the contented calm of play from the ominous silence that warns of trouble.

A husband is listened to only against the drama of day watch and night watch. The ever-present policewoman is whistling on her beat, twirling a stick, her flat shoes sounding on the pavement.

—Karen Mains
West Chicago, Illinois

You Teach Me
What Matters

As mothers, we must teach our children everything—how to hold a spoon, how to tie shoelaces, how to offer a gentle hug when they've hurt their sister. Yet throughout their growing-up years, our children also teach us lessons we soon learn to cherish. Let the tender insights on these next pages hug you as you reflect on what really matters.

You just held my hand and walked me up the stairs. I thought about hurrying you as my mind sorted through the ten things to get done once you were down for a nap but then there I sat, trapped between your warm body and the back of that rocking chair, and the list suddenly seemed insignificant. It was a moment of true contentment—needing and loving measured by soft hums and quiet breathing. Thank you for all you teach, Miss Rylee. I love you.

—Jami Lyn Weber, Sisters, Oregon

A mother is someone who dreams for you, but then lets you chase the dreams you have for yourself and loves you just the same.

—Author unkown

✻　　✻　　✻

AS YOU PLAY, I WATCH YOUR WONDER AND JOY at the simplest of things—the wind blowing leaves, a hummingbird hovering over a flower. Suddenly the whole world is put in perspective. Thank you for reminding me how good life really is.

—**Michelle Lewis**, Phoenix, Arizona

ONE MORNING WHEN I WAS CRYING OVER the news of the death of a friend and thinking of the pain her two little boys must be suffering, my son, Alex, in his concerned toddler voice, asked me why I was crying. I hugged him close and explained that someone very important and loved by many people had gone home to God. He hugged me back and said, "No, Mommy, you're still here."

—**Dawn Lewis**, Glendora, California

MOTHERHOOD IS LIKE CLIMBING A MOUNTAIN. Some days the peak seems miles away, and I want to turn around and forget about my goal of reaching the top. But other days, the climbing is quick and easy, and I see myself and my children atop the mountain. My children are birds, and I am letting them go. We did it. I did it. God did it. I wouldn't change that mountain trek for a cruise any day.

—**Angela Dean Lund**, Sisters, Oregon

WHEN YOU COME INTO MY ROOM TO TALK about your troubles—and it always seems to be late at night—I've learned you don't really want answers. You just want someone who will listen to each word, and understand, and care. In other words, a mom.

—**Betty Lund**, Eugene, Oregon

ONE HOT JULY MORNING, I AWOKE TO THE clicks of a broken fan blowing humid air across my face. The well-used fan had seen better days. It had only one setting, and its blades were worn and bent. It needed repair. So, I thought, did my life.

Earlier that year, Sarah, our Down's syndrome daughter, had undergone heart surgery. That was behind us, but now we faced mounting medical bills that insurance wouldn't cover. On top of that, my husband's job would be eliminated in just weeks, and losing our home seemed inevitable.

As I closed my eyes to try to put together a morning prayer, I felt a small hand nudge my arm. "Mommy," Sarah said, "I g-g-got r-r-ready for v-v-vacation B-B-Bible school all by myself!"

Next to the bed stood five-year-old Sarah, her eyes twinkling through thick, pink-framed glasses. Beaming, she turned both palms up and exclaimed, "Ta-dah!"

Her red-checked, seersucker shorts were on backward, with the drawstring stuck in the side waistband. A J. C. Penney price tag hung from a new, green polka-dot top. It was inside out. She had chosen one red and one green winter sock to go with the outfit. Her tennis shoes were on the wrong feet, and she wore a baseball cap with the visor and emblem turned backward.

"I-I-I packed a b-b-backpack, t-t-too!" she stuttered while unzipping her bag so I could see what was inside. Curious, I peered in at the treasures she had so carefully packed: five Lego blocks, an unopened box of paper clips, a fork, a naked Cabbage Patch doll, three jigsaw puzzle pieces, and a crib sheet from the linen closet.

Gently lifting her chin until our eyes met, I said very slowly, "You look beautiful!"

"Thank y-y-you." Sarah smiled as she began to twirl around like a ballerina.

Just then the living room clocked chimed eight, which meant I had forty-five minutes to get Sarah, a toddler, and a baby out the door. As I hurried to feed the kids while rocking a crying infant, the morning minutes dissolved into urgent seconds. I knew I was not going to have time to change Sarah's outfit.

Buckling each child into a car seat, I tried to reason with Sarah. "Honey, I don't think you'll be needing your backpack for vacation Bible school. Why don't you let me keep it in the car for you."

"No-o-o-o-o. I n-n-need it!"

I finally surrendered, telling myself her self-esteem was more important than what people might think of her backpack full of useless stuff. When we got to the church, I attempted to redo Sarah's outfit with one hand while I held my baby in the other. But Sarah pulled away, reminding me of my early morning words, "No-o-o-o…I look beautiful!"

Overhearing our conversation, a young teacher joined us. "You do look beautiful!" the woman told Sarah. Then she took Sarah's hand and said to me, "You can pick up Sarah at 11:30. We'll take good care of her." As I watched them walk away, I knew Sarah was in good hands.

While Sarah was in school, I took the other two children and ran errands. As I dropped late payments into the mailbox and shopped with coupons at the grocery store, my thoughts raced with anxiety and disjointed prayer. What did the future hold? How would we provide for our three small children? Would we lose our home? Did God really care about us?

I got back to the church a few minutes early. A door to the sun-filled chapel had been propped open, and I could see the children seated inside in a semicircle listening to a Bible story.

Sarah, sitting with her back to me, was still clutching the canvas straps that secured her backpack. Her baseball cap, shorts, and shirt were still on backward and inside out.

As I watched her, one simple thought came to mind: "I sure do love her."

And as I stood there, I heard that still, comforting voice that I have come to understand is God's: "That's the way I feel about you."

I closed my eyes and imagined my Creator looking at me from a distance: my life so much like Sarah's outfit—backward, unmatched, mixed up.

"Why are you holding that useless 'backpack' full of anxiety, doubt, and fear?" I could imagine God saying to me. "Let me carry it."

That night as I once again turned on our crippled fan, I felt a renewed sense of hope. Sarah had reminded me that God's presence remains even when life needs repair. She had been a messenger of God's love. What a privilege to parent such a child.

— **Nancy Jo Sullivan**, St. Paul, Minnesota

TENDERLY I TUCK THE LAST CHILD INTO bed, step over toys, and make my way down the hall toward my bedroom. Exhausted, I fall into bed and begin to reflect upon the day. The simple construction paper cards covered with hearts, glue, and glitter, and the crayon words spelling, "I love you, Mommy," caress my own heart as I fall asleep praying:

O Lord, the Mother's Day cards and sticky kisses are warm expressions of love that I shall treasure always. They make me even more determined to be a better mom. But as much as I try, I can't seem to get it all done. It's been a busy day, as are all of our days. Stories are left unread, and prayers are left unsaid as we juggle our daily schedules. The toys strewn over the house, the laundry waiting to be folded, the bathrooms screaming to be cleaned, and the bills to be paid gnaw at the corners of my mind.

As I check on my children sleeping peacefully in their beds, their innocence, vulnerability, and dependence upon me almost overwhelm me. I need Your strength and wisdom, Lord.

I want to be a mother who is never too busy to work puzzles, throw rocks in the creek, and splash in the puddles with them. O Lord, remind me of my priorities. May I choose the love and admiration of my children over the acclaim of the world.

Be my energy when I'm tired and fill me with a sense of humor. I want my little ones to remember my laughter, praise, and prayers. May they rest peacefully each night knowing that I love them and You love them, too! In Jesus' name, amen.

—Edwina Patterson, Plano, Texas

GOD GIVES US BEAUTIFUL GIFTS. FOR ME, ONE is being a mother.

—Susan Petrovits, Kodiak, Alaska

BAD NEWS IS STILL WELCOME NEWS WHEN IT'S my daughter on the phone. It means we're still in touch.

—Sandi Hansen, Longview, Washington

MY SWEET DREAMS FOR YOU

We mothers are encouragers, cheerleaders, and visionaries in a single package. We bandage our children's hurts today and see the wondrous potential of their tomorrows. We are optimists and dreamers by definition—for we are mothers, always seeking the very best for the precious ones in our midst. Read on to discover the abiding presence of a mother's hope.

The time? Midnight. My gown? A fuzzy robe. The music? A quiet radio. The lighting? Dim glow of the digital clock. My partner? A little bald man only three months old. We swing and sway in each other's arms as the night ticks by, oblivious to the rest of the world. My restless partner melts into my chest and we become one...again. Tonight I dream of a night on the town. Someday, my dreams will be of kitchen dancing.

—**Susan Rockwell**, Grandville, Michigan

Who but your mother shares your moments of glory? Who else sees you at your weakest and most vulnerable and picks you up, helping you grow strong? Your mom believes in your dreams, even when they lie in tatters at your feet. She picks you up and helps you dream again.

—Author unknown

To be a mother is the grandest vocation in the world. No one being has a position of such power and influence. She holds in her hands the destiny of nations.

—Hannah Whitall Smith

I MARVEL. FAINT FLUTTERS OF MOVEMENT. An intoxicating, pink-lotioned head. Teething and toddling. Five-year-old frankness. Elementary antics, good and bad. Junior high jitters. Osmotic parental pain and insecurities. High school headiness. Readiness? Cars, late nights, I worry. Dating, peer pressure, I worry. Glimmers of independence. The blink of an eye. Cap, gown, tassel. The world beckons. I let go.

—Mary Jedlicka Humston, Iowa City, Iowa

49

My two sons, I always wanted you.

Even when I was a little girl playing with baby dolls.

I clothed them and fed them, rocked them and sang a lullaby,

Thinking that one day I would have babes of my own.

And God gave me you,
My two sons.
And I clothed you and fed you,
I rocked you to sleep
And sang you a lullaby.
And it was wonderful.
I wanted it to last
Forever.

But quickly you grew older,
With sturdy legs and grinning faces.
And we made a sandbox,
Played with Legos,
And read stories.
We learned to ride bikes,
And mended owies.
And you grew up.

Now you are young men.
Both over six feet tall,
with whiskers.
It feels like you don't need me
very much.
And I have to let go.
And trust God to care for you,
But it's the hardest thing I've ever done.

My two sons,
I always wanted you.
But now all I can do
Is watch and pray,
That you will let God
Clothe you and feed you,
Rock you and sing you a lullaby.
And it will be wonderful.

—**Melody Carlson**, Sisters, Oregon

Little children are still the symbol of the eternal marriage between love and duty.

—George Eliot

Children dear, if our lives are loving, Sweet to all like the clover here,

Having the modest grace of violets, Full of the buttercup's sunny cheer,

We shall be God's little human flowers, Helping to brighten this world of ours.

—Caro A. Dugan

YOU'RE SLEEPING NOW AT LAST. SOME DAYS I think this nighttime peace will never come. I love my days with you. Your reliable smile was the only thing that lit up this frantic house today, Max.

Zachary, I sometimes think that if I had half your energy and persistence, I'd accomplish miracles in minutes. But loving my days with you as I do, I have a motherly confession to make—I love the hour you fall asleep as well.

—Mary Fisher, Nyack, New York

I AM WATCHING AS MY OLDEST CHILD IS getting ready for her first day of kindergarten, and I see the first of so many steps. I want to hold her back and keep her little for just a while longer, but I know I cannot tie her down. For tomorrow she will be that young college grad off to conquer the world. I just pray that I am ready when she is.

—Vicki Aardema
Alexandria, Virginia

HIS LOVE IS PERFECT

A mother's love is truly like no other—yet there is One whose love transcends even our soul-deep feelings for our children. His is a love we can know and rely on, a love that offers comfort and confidence, a love that is complete and perfect. Cherish the words of mothers who have put their trust in an all-knowing, all-loving God, the Creator of every child.

Today I didn't say the right things. I didn't give enough hugs. I didn't listen to all of their imaginary stories. Today I hurried them through what could have been very special moments to achieve my binding agenda. Today my prayers were too short and my lectures too long. My smiles, I'm sure, didn't hide my fatigue. Today I didn't heal any wounds; in fact, I'm sure I caused some. Their tears fell, and I felt too lifeless to wipe them away. Today I felt completely defeated and totally inadequate for this position called "mommy."

But as I kneel in prayer to confess my failure, I am reminded...I am not their hope. I am not their total joy. I am not their salvation. He is! And they are His children even more than they are

Children are a gift from God.

—Psalm 127:3, TLB

You made all the delicate, inner parts of my body, and knit them together in my mother's womb. Thank you for making me so wonderfully complex! It is amazing to think about. Your workmanship is marvelous.

—Psalm 139:13-14 TLB

mine. I am reminded...He always listens, always guides, always touches, and always loves perfectly. I can rest now, Lord, remembering that I am not alone.

—**Wendy C. Brewer,** Fairview Heights, Illinois

GOD MIRACULOUSLY SENDS THE RIGHT CHILD to the right mother. Nick and I like to count through all his cousins and friends and marvel that they all ended up with just the right mother.

—**Miriam Brownlee,** Philadelphia, Pennsylvania

I PRAY MY KIDS KNOW YOU DEEPLY, IN SPITE of me. For their sakes, Father, don't give up on me. Change my heart!

—**Rhonda Johnson,** Norman, Oklahoma

I ADOPTED MY DAUGHTER, KATIE, FROM China when she was only nine months old, and I was forty-seven and single. A case of middle-aged insanity? Not on your life! The moment I held her in my arms I knew Someone Really Big had brought us together.

—**Ann Spangler,** Belmont, Michigan

As a mother comforts her child, so will I comfort you.

—Isaiah 66:13

USUALLY THE MOON SHINES BRIGHT ON clear May nights in eastern Pennsylvania. But tonight the moon is missing. All is dark. I notice brown circles under the lamp in the hall when Mother welcomes our 2:00 A.M. arrival from Illinois. I also notice brown circles under her eyes. Spots I'd never noticed before. Tired skin under gentle folds.

But here she stands, my mother of forty years. I sense an accumulation of nights waiting up for home-coming children, as though the years have cast shadows from the lamp onto her face. I see the years in the black and blue veins that have just this week felt the heart specialist's probe. I hear the years—like the ocean ringing in a seashell—in the doctor's diagnosis: "Red flag…enlarged heart…slow the pace…." I stare into uncertainty. Mother has been a steady pulse throughout the years. Tomorrow has been an assumed promise a grand procession of family weddings, births,

graduations, music recitals, ordinations, Christmas, Easter, Thanksgiving. Time has been an event, not a sequence.

As I look at Mother, I sense that someone has wound the clock. Time now has a cadence. Years have become increments. History has a beginning and an end. I shiver in the early morning chill. But then Mother's arms wrap me in warmth, and I am home. A forty-year-old child reassured by her mother's touch. There is no time in touch. Welcoming arms know not the years.

I hear the teakettle whistling. Freshly baked chocolate chip cookies wait on the old ironstone plate that once served cookies from Grandma Hollinger's kitchen. Mother's chocolate chip cookies and Grandma Hollinger's ironstone plate pull me back into timelessness. We sip peppermint tea and laugh over a silly story Dad tells. Our laughter drowns out the clock. There is

Maternal love! Thou word that sums all bliss.

—Robert Pollock

no time in laughter. Mother laughs the hardest of all. Dark circles. Tired circles of joy. Her children are home.

For a moment I forget bruised veins and ticking clocks. I am held together by things that do not change—a mother's early welcome, freshly baked chocolate chip cookies, an ironstone plate, peppermint tea, a mantel clock, and laughter. I am held together by a God who does not change. I know the God of time who is yet above time. I see tonight in my mother's face the strange paradox of time and timelessness. A rare glimpse of the divine.

—**Ruth Senter,** Lake Forest, Illinois

I WAS SPELLBOUND AT BECOMING A MOTHER. How could God trust me so?

—**Barbra Gordonnter,** Chappaqua, New York

SUDDENLY I REALIZE THAT THE SHEER intensity of my love cannot protect this child from the perils of life. Spinal meningitis. Playground tragedies. Traffic accidents. God, I can't stand it. My chest constricts with unborn grief. My breath comes quickly. To risk love is to risk loss. Shadows stretch across the living room and across my mind. And then I hear it. The still, small voice saying gently, deep inside, "You're not a proud new owner. You're a trusted caretaker. This is my child, and I've lent him to you. Love him dearly, but hold him freely. Trust me for the days ahead."

—**Sandra Bernlehr Clark**
New Brighton, Minnesota

I HOLD YOU IN MY ARMS, YOUNG PRINCE. You sleep in sweet, heavenly peace. Yet, I wonder if you'd be so calm if you knew the truth: I am your mother. And I don't have the slightest idea what I'm doing.

In the hospital I had to be instructed on how to nurse you. Yesterday my mother showed me how to bathe you in the sink. I don't have a clue

Motherhood is a partnership with God.

—Author unknown

how to clear up diaper rash. I get queasy at the sight of blood. I don't sew. My math skills are atrocious. And you might as well know right up front—wiggly teeth give me the heebie-jeebies.

However, I am very good at baking cookies. I know how to make indoor tents on rainy days. And I have my father's wonderful sense of humor, so I know how to laugh and how to make you laugh.

I'll sing you sweet songs in the night. I'll pray for you every day. I'll let you keep any animal you catch, as long as you feed it. I'll call all your imaginary friends by their first names. I'll put love notes in your lunch box, and I'll swim with you in the ocean, even when I'm old.

To me, these tender intuitions are what matter most. Eternal insights only a mother can know—when her baby is in her arms, as you are now in mine. This is where the Lord will teach me how to mother you by heart.

—**Robin Jones Gunn**, Vancouver, Washington

LORD,

When they scribble on the walls, please help me to see a rainbow!

And when I've said something a hundred times, please give me the patience to say it a hundred times more!

And on those particularly annoying days when I tell them to act their age, please help me to remember that they are!

And while we're on the subject of age, Lord, when I begin to lose my temper, please help me to remember to act mine!

And through it all, Lord—the fingerprints and runny noses, messy rooms and unrolled toilet paper, destroyed videotapes and broken knickknacks—please help me to remember this: someday, these will be the days I will long to have back again!

—**Angela Thole**, Bloomington, Minnesota

ACKNOWLEDGMENTS

From the lips of children and infants you have ordained praise.

— Psalm 8:2

I'LL LOVE YOU FOREVER

Angela Dean Lund. Used by permission of the author.

Pam Svoboda. Used by permission of the author.

Theresa Meyers. Theresa is a nationally published writer and
mother of two toddlers in Port Orchard, Washington.
You can find her on the Web at www.theresa.meyers.com.

Carla Risener Bresnahan. Used by permission of the author.

Elisa Morgan and Carol Kuykendall. From *What Every Child
Needs* by Elisa Morgan and Carol Kuykendall.
Copyright © 1997 by M.O.P.S. International, Inc.
Used by permission of Zondervan Publishing House.

Janet Chambers. Used by permission of the author.

Linda Crawford. Used by permission of the author.

Sarah Keeton. Used by permission of the author.

Patricia Sprinkle. Used by permission of the author.

Carla Schneider. Used by permission of the author.

Rebecca Stephens. Used by permission of the author.

Kathy Erickson. Used by permission of the author.

YOU BRING ME SUCH JOY

Gina Barrett Schlesinger dedicates her story to the memory
of her mother, Alma Barrett.

Barbi Townsend. Used by permission of the author.

Dawn Lewis. Used by permission of the author.

Juanita Tamayo Lott. Juanita is married to Robert Henry Lott.
They are proud parents of David Tamayo Lott and
Joseph Henry Lot III.

Elisa Morgan. Used by permission of the author.

Debbie Ricker. Used by permission of the author.

Tonya Roberts. Used by permission of the author.

Martha Manning. From *Chasing Grace* © 1997.
Reprinted by permission of Harper Collins Publishers, Inc.

Mary Byrne Santori. Used by permission of the author.

Vickey L. Banks. Vickey Banks is the happily married mother of
two terrific children who truly treasures the relationships in her
life. She is an inspirational speaker and author of *Love Letters
to My Baby* (Multnomah Publishers, Inc.).

Madeleine L'Engle. Reprinted from *Mothers & Daughters* © 1977
by Madeleine L'Engle. Used by permission of Waterbrook
Press, Colorado Springs, CO. All rights reserved.